THE
SECRETS OF
SPIRITUAL
HEALING

*A Beginner's Guide
to Energy Therapies*

ELSIE WILD

summersdale

CONTENTS

*Wellness is the complete
integration of body, mind, and
spirit... everything we do, think,
feel, and believe has an effect
on our state of well-being.*

GREG ANDERSON

INTRODUCTION

There are a lot of buzzwords surrounding the culture of healing and wellness. You can't read a magazine these days without finding something about alternative medicine or the latest well-being trend, or perhaps auras, chakras or the herbs that should be in your tea. The term "spiritual healing" may raise a few eyebrows, but what exactly is it? And does it work?

Spiritual healing, also known as energy healing, is a method of treating the physical body and the mind using alternative medicines to improve our overall health and quality of life. While the words "spiritual" and "soul" will appear a lot throughout this book, you don't have to be religious in order to try spiritual healing (although it can be a religious experience if you choose it to be). "Spirit" is simply another term for your body's natural energies or your emotional state.

This book will start you off on your journey, introducing you to new healing practices, while giving you guidance and tips. It will explain the many types of healing and uncover the mysteries that surround each practice so you can try them for yourself. It is also designed to help you become more connected with your body and soul, so that you can start feeling your best self.

A quick note before we begin our quest to spiritual healing and better health. While we will be talking about alternative medicines and practices to improve your health, it's important to remember that spiritual healing should be performed in addition to any medicinal treatments you are currently receiving. It should not be used as a replacement for medicine, surgery, vaccines, chemotherapy, counselling or psychiatry. It's also very important to talk to a doctor you trust before performing any of the healing practices in this book.

This book will help you listen to your body and figure out what it needs from you. This will be different for everyone, so the focus here is on treating symptoms – especially emotional symptoms – rather than specific illnesses or diseases.

However, you may notice that throughout this book there is mention of depression and anxiety, which are sometimes symptoms of other major physical and mental health issues. Spiritual healing cannot cure depression or anxiety, but it can alleviate them to a degree and may help to make episodes shorter, less frequent or more bearable.

Spiritual healing is about listening to your body's needs and becoming intuitive to the energy that flows within you. Once your energies become balanced, things will start to fall into place and you should feel more happy, healthy and radiant.

Now, let the journey begin.

Chapter One:

EXPLORING YOUR ENERGIES

Quantum physics has helped us understand that everything in life is made up of energy, from the chair we sit in to the air we breathe. Energy powers the world and our lives. Our bodies use energy every day to keep us alive. We use energy to move from one place to another and when we use our brains to solve complex problems. We gain energy when we eat and when we have a good night's sleep. Our energy – and the energy of the world – is flowing all the time, even if we cannot see it.

In addition to the energy already flowing through our daily lives, we also have another form that is felt deep down in our core called spiritual energy.

Spiritual energy is the manifestation of our life force. It is what keeps us energized and connected to both the physical world and the spiritual realm. When we are happy, when we feel loved, when we are feeling ourselves and stepping into our power, we are feeling the highest vibration of our spiritual energy.

However, there are days when we do not feel our best. Perhaps you feel completely drained and don't know the reason why. Perhaps you suddenly feel angry although there's no cause for it. This could be because you didn't sleep properly, or it's been raining for too long, or you aren't feeling well. However, if these feelings and moods continue, perhaps it's your spiritual energies that have shifted off balance.

The term "off balance" comes up a lot when we talk about energy and spirituality, but what does it really mean? When we say "balanced", we mean that our energies are at the perfect level to allow us to do everything we need, feel content and be able to reach our full potential. If our energies are too low, we could become sad, ill and unable to grow. Too high and we can be too active and unable to focus on our growth. When we are balanced, we are aligned with our energies and to our highest purpose in life.

This is why having a balanced spiritual energy is important: when our energy is off we need a way to become balanced again. This is where energy healing comes in.

Energy or spiritual healing is a holistic practice that activates the body's spiritual energy system to remove negative energy blocks. Breaking down and releasing these blocks allows the body to start healing itself – physically, mentally, emotionally and spiritually. When we start healing, we can begin growing.

🪷 ENERGY BLOCKS AND 🪷 ENERGY VAMPIRES

Energy blocks, also referred to as emotional blocks, are emotions and feelings that prevent us from growing, healing and taking on the energy we need. Think of them as invisible wounds that are stored in our body's energy fields. When these wounds stay open, all of our energy leaks out. Energy blocks come in many forms: internal blocks could be caused by trauma, anxiety, depression, physical or mental stress, abuse, low self-worth or limiting beliefs. External blocks could take the form of environmental stresses (things in the world around you that trigger negative feelings), malnutrition, substance abuse and lack of exercise.

People can also be a source of energy blocks. In healthy relationships, people give and take energy to and from the other person in order to nurture and help each other grow. In unhealthy relationships, one person does all the giving while the other does all the taking until the giver is drained dry. The taker in a relationship is called an "energy vampire" because they suck all the energy out of you. These vampires can show up in various forms: a demanding boss, an ungrateful friend, a controlling parent, an unsupportive partner. You can never become spiritually healed unless you cut these energy vampires out of your life.

However, it's not always enough to get out of a toxic relationship or remove yourself from a harmful environment – you still need to do the spiritual healing in order to get your energy back and become balanced once more.

🪷 GOOD VIBES ONLY 🪷

You've probably seen the phrase "good vibes" in various forms on social media, T-shirts and products, but what does it really mean? What are vibes and why should we care if they're good or not?

Something else physics has taught us is that matter is comprised of molecules, each with its own vibrations. Even something as solid as a desk is always vibrating and humans are always vibrating, too. While we cannot see these vibrations with our eyes or feel them with our touch, we can feel the *energy* the vibrations give off. Think of the way we know that our co-worker is in a bad mood just by how the energy shifts in their presence. When we meet someone cheerful and positive, we cannot help but smile. We feed off each other's vibrations. So, when we talk about "good vibes" we are really talking about vibrational energy. People who are content and at peace with the world tend to vibrate on a higher frequency than those who are unhappy and have unresolved energy blocks.

Places also have vibrations attached to them. If we feel a little odd or uncomfortable when we first walk into a room – something that you couldn't explain other than feeling "bad vibes" – chances are something happened in that room to give it a negative vibration.

One of the many reasons why lots of people's favourite place is the beach is because of all the good vibrations present. The salt in the sea cleanses all the negativity from the shore and the moving air keeps the good vibrations coming.

A BRIEF HISTORY OF SPIRITUAL HEALING

Spiritual healing has taken many forms in many different cultures. As long as there have been humans, there have been people trying to heal them. Spiritual healing has roots in ancient Egypt, Babylon, Greece, Jerusalem and China, back when medical "professionals" were trained through oral tradition, while many thought the gods played a hand in choosing healers. Each culture had its own system for spiritual healing and their own words for the energy that flows through us.

In ancient India, the Hindu philosophy spoke about a universal energy called *prana,* a Sanskrit word for "breath". Prana is believed to be the source of all life and moves through all forms to give the breath of life. Prana moves through the seven energetic building blocks of the mind and body, which are called chakras. When the chakras work together in harmony, they bring the person enlightenment and spiritual wellness. However, if prana levels are low in the chakra, all the other chakras can become unbalanced.

Ancient China (as far back as the fifth century BC) had its own version of prana called *ch'i* or *qi,* which translates as "air". Qi is the circulating life energy that is present in all things. Those who study Chinese traditional medicine believe that qi is made up of two polar forces: yin and yang. When yin and yang are balanced, the body and the spirit are healthy; when they are not, then the spirit is unwell. Acupuncture and herbal cures are supposed to balance out yin and yang.

Over the centuries various forms of spiritual healing have been practised, from faith healing in Christian churches where healers place their hands on a person's head to heal them; to Japan's own version of energy healing called reiki, which was founded in the early twentieth century. While these methods are very different, they all involve transferring one person's energy to another in an effort to heal.

HOW IS SPIRITUAL HEALING PRACTISED?

There are many ways that spiritual healing can be practised. Some of these practices can be performed yourself while others will require a specialist. Whether you are meditating in the comforts of your own home or receiving an acupuncture treatment, as long as the energy is flowing, spiritual healing can happen.

It's important to note that your energy and spirit may not be immediately healed after one session of spiritual healing. Sometimes energy blocks are so large, they will take time to heal, so don't be discouraged if you don't feel completely better after your first attempt. If after a few tries a particular practice is still not working for you, try another. Keep putting in that energy and your emotional wounds will begin to heal.

Chapter Two:
YOUR HEALING TOOLKIT

Before you can begin your journey into spiritual healing, you're going to need the right tools for the job. A plumber can't fix a leaky pipe without their tool belt and you cannot heal your energy leaks without the proper equipment. As you go through this chapter, and the rest of the book, highlight things you may need for the kinds of spiritual healing you intend to try. Remember this kind of healing is not one size fits all. Not every tool will work for every person, so be open to experimenting.

It's also important to remember that you do not need to spend much money on your tools for them to work. A witching stick made from a stick you found in your backyard can work just as well as an expensive one. As long as you put your energy in, it will work. As you go through this chapter, think about some budget-friendly switches you can make.

Here are some handy tools to put into your healing toolkit.

✿ CRYSTALS ✿

Crystals can be very useful tools when it comes to healing work, thanks to the energy vibrations they carry. Crystals come from the earth, and objects that come from nature are believed to carry special properties that can aid healing, improve balance and increase energy.

The concept of using stones or crystals as talismans or amulets has been around almost since the dawn of time. The first known use of crystals for healing was around 4000 BC by the Sumerians in Mesopotamia. The Sumerians carved images representing a person's life on to crystals such as gypsum and haematite, which they would leave in temples, believing they had protective properties. In ancient Egypt, members of royalty would wear certain crystals to honour their favourite gods and goddesses. Some Egyptians were buried with quartz on their forehead for safe travels into the afterlife. Ancient Asian cultures believed that the mind, body and spirit are all connected through qi (life force) and divided up into energy centres known as chakras, and that if you placed a healing crystal on a certain chakra, it would increase the positive energy and heal that area.

Crystals can be used in various ways. You can place them on your chakras to energize them, hold them while meditating, carry them with you or wear them as jewellery, or keep them in your home or office. While you can use any crystal that speaks to you, here are some that are the best for spiritual healing:

- **AMETHYST**: Promotes inner calm, helps with decision-making and opening the third eye.
- **AGATE**: Promotes grounding and stability.
- **CARNELIAN**: Encourages creativity and vitality.
- **JASPER**: Brings joy and stress relief.
- **LAPIS LAZULI**: Encourages wisdom and self-awareness.
- **TURQUOISE**: Protects against negative energy.

🪷 WITCHING STICK 🪷

Dowsing is a form of divination traditionally used to find water, metals or gemstones, but can also be used to find and heal negative energy in a practice known as energy dowsing. Dowsing works by using a Y-shaped stick known as a witching stick. Witching sticks are usually made of wood, but can also be formed from copper suspended by nylon or silk thread.

To practise energy dowsing, take your witching stick and slowly move it over your entire body. If the witching stick moves, your energy may be off and your chakra or aura might need to be cleansed and realigned.

🪷 PENDULUM 🪷

Like the witching stick, a pendulum can be used for dowsing and is much easier to carry around with you. A pendulum is a symmetrical, weighted object that is hung from a single chain or cord. You can use anything you like as your pendulum: a rock, wooden ball or glass marble, for instance. As long as it's not magnetic, it's good to go.

Pendulums are used in energy dowsing to see where your energy might be blocked and to help realign your chakras. However, you can also use your pendulum to ask questions to guide you.

If you've never used a pendulum before, you're going to need to program it first. Programming your pendulum means telling it what signals it should give when answering your questions. For example: hold the pendulum out in front of you and say, "When I ask a question and the answer is 'yes', move back and forth" and move the pendulum back and forth as you say this. Do the same for "no" and "maybe".

Say you were wondering if herbal healing is right for you. You would sit down, pick up your pendulum by the chain and hold it out in front of you. Clear your mind and ask your question. The way the pendulum moves will give you your answer, according to how you've programmed it.

✿ ESSENTIAL OILS ✿

Essential oils are compounds extracted from plants, capturing their scent and "essence". Because the oil has the essence of the plant, it also harnesses its energy, which can be transferred to the user. Certain essential oils can balance energies, clear negativity, relieve stress and improve emotional healing.

There are many ways to incorporate essential oils into your healing process. You can pour a few drops into a diffuser during your meditation, put diluted oil in a balm to use in a massage or even dab diluted essential oil on to the pulse points of your skin, as you would perfume.

There is a large variety of essential oils to choose from, so here are a few recommended for healing and rebalancing:

- **CYPRESS:** Promotes stability.
- **LAVENDER:** Helps with calming and balance.
- **LEMONGRASS:** Good for calming and clearing your thoughts.
- **PEPPERMINT:** Promotes clear thinking.
- **ROSEMARY:** Improves mental clarity.
- **SANDALWOOD:** Good for meditation and opening your mind.

Before putting anything on or into your body, please do the research. If you have allergies or sensitive skin, do not use essential oils without talking to your doctor first. Do not put undiluted essential oil directly on to your skin, or you could get a chemical burn. If you are a pet owner, be careful which essential oil you put in to your diffuser as some are highly toxic to pets. Do not use your diffuser in an enclosed, windowless space with your pet for hours at a time. And remember that with oils, as with most things in life, a little goes a long way.

🪷 SALT 🪷

Yes, this simple household seasoning holds incredible power when it comes to your healing process. If you're looking to cleanse your aura quickly, a pinch of sea salt or pink Himalayan salt will do the trick. Salt is important to your toolkit for the same reason it's important to keep in your kitchen – it enhances the overall effect of what you're creating.

Salt is associated with purity and protection, and is commonly used to banish bad vibrations and protect you from harmful energies. There is even a form of salt therapy called halotherapy where a person meditates in a salt cave or salt room, allowing the dry air to cleanse their body and mind.

But if you don't have the salt requirements to create your own cave, there are other ways to use salt in your practice. Try casting a salt circle around you while you are meditating to keep out negative energies, plugging in a Himalayan salt lamp to filter out negative vibrations or taking a sea-salt soak in a bath to cleanse your aura.

❧ SINGING BOWL ❧

A singing bowl, also known as a "sound bowl" or "praying bowl", is an inverted bell that looks similar to a bowl, typically made of copper alloy or crystal. When tapped or pressed firmly with a mallet, the bell vibrates and produces a rich, deep sound. Some believe the sound can create vibrations that help to reduce stress in the body while harmonizing the cells, creating balance in your energy system. The tones created by the singing bowl are also associated with different chakra centres.

Singing bowls date back to ancient China and Mongolia, where they were used as gongs. Tibetan Buddhist monks have used singing bowls during their meditation practices to rebalance their energies during meditation. The popularity of singing bowls started to rise in the 1970s when they were used in New Age music. Groovy.

A singing bowl can be used during meditation to clear your mind and balance your energy. It can also help to realign your chakras. Singing bowls are used in sound therapy as some claim that the tone of the bell can produce beneficial changes in the brainwaves.

To use a singing bowl, take your mallet and press it against the outer rim of the bowl, moving it in a circular motion using your full arm, until you hear a clear tone. Then slow down but continue to move your mallet in a circular motion.

🪷 AN OPEN MIND 🪷

Finally, the most important thing you'll need is an open mind. You can have all the best tools, but if you come in with the wrong mindset thinking "this will never work", it won't. You cannot heal yourself if you are in a negative headspace. Thoughts are actions. Not everything will work for you, or work on the first try. But if you come into this with an open mind and heart, you are already on the path to wellness.

Chapter Three:
SPIRITUAL HEALING PRACTICES

Now to the fun part, the actual spiritual practices themselves. This section will look at each method of spirituality, starting with those you can do by yourself and moving into those you should do with the help of a professional (please do not try acupuncture on yourself!). This section also categorizes healing practices that go together. For example, all practices that are associated with chakras are grouped together, while those falling under traditional Chinese medicine follow one after the other.

You don't have to read this section in order, you can easily skip around and read the subjects that interest you, returning to other subjects later. Much like the actual art of spiritual healing, this can be done at your own pace, however you see fit.

So, let's get started.

✿ MOON HEALING ✿

Life is a continuous cycle and nothing teaches us that quite like the moon, which goes through several stages of being whole and bright before fading into the darkness and transforming all over again. Like us, the moon goes through periods of lightness and darkness, but it keeps on going regardless.

The moon has always had a pull on us, literally, as it is the force behind the tides of our oceans. It also affects the cycles of nature. Certain animals are more active during a full moon, while weather is more intense during the new moon. Humans have also long been affected by the moon, and it has been the subject of mythology and folklore for millennia. In astrology, the moon represents our ever-changing emotions and moods, our internal needs, our unconscious behaviours and our intuition. In witchcraft, witches try to harness the moon's natural magic by performing spells during certain phases of the moon to give them an extra kick.

Just as each phase in our lives is important in its own way, each phase of the 29.5-day lunar cycle has its own characteristic that we can use in our lives and in our own healing practices. Many spiritual healers will wait until a certain moon phase to unblock a chakra or before a healing ritual in order to get the full benefits from the moon. Some people use a lunar cycle tracker on their phone or purchase a lunar phase planner to keep track of the moon's phases and make plans accordingly. By living by the lunar cycle, our energies become balanced and more aligned with our best selves.

If you are interested in living your life by the lunar cycle and what it can do for you, take a look at each moon phase listed below, as well as their meanings, and start planning.

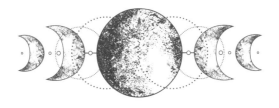

New moon

REPRESENTS: New beginnings, clarity, reflection, cleansing.

WHAT IT DOES: With the new moon we are able to let go of our past, and embrace a renewal of energy and possibilities. This is the time to plant the seeds for your dreams of a healthy, better life. In the darkest time, we have hope that light will come again and we will regain full power once more.

HOW TO USE THIS ENERGY: Spend some time alone to set goals. What do you want to achieve? What results do you wish to see within yourself? Where do you want to be during the next new moon? Recharge your internal batteries and refocus on yourself.

Waxing crescent moon

REPRESENTS: Motivation, attraction, success.

WHAT IT DOES: As we begin to see the light of the moon, we begin to see that our goals may indeed be possible. The first shoots of our seedlings are coming out. The waxing moon expands our energy, motivation and our ability to focus. It encourages us to be self-confident and put ourselves in social situations.

HOW TO USE THIS ENERGY: Start actively setting intentions of what you want. If you have a spiritual healing practice picked out, now is the time to begin. Tell the universe what you want and begin attracting what you desire.

 First quarter half-moon

REPRESENTS: Creativity, calm, intuition.

WHAT IT DOES: At this phase we are refocusing on our goals and making sure we are heading in the right direction, based on what our intuition is telling us to do. This is where we gain strength and creative energy. The half-moon removes doubt from our heart, assuring us that we are going in the right direction.

HOW TO USE THIS ENERGY: Roll up your sleeves and get to work by taking a deep dive into creative projects you are excited about (painting, writing, singing, etc.). Re-evaluate your plans, meditate on where you are in life and make decisions. Don't give up!

Waxing gibbous moon

REPRESENTS: Observation, health, gaining.

WHAT IT DOES: This is where you start seeing the fruits of your labour. The feeling of almost being complete and recharged. It gives us time to reflect on where we have been and how far we need to go. Edit your plans if things aren't working out, but stay the course.

HOW TO USE THIS ENERGY: Organize your environment to tidy up your mental space. Don't fight your feelings – if they're telling you to change direction, do not resist. Go with your flowing energies.

Full moon

REPRESENTS: Power, healing, charging, clarity.

WHAT IT DOES: We have finally reached our full power and are reaping the benefits of the seeds we have sown. Emotions will be felt more strongly than normal. If your vibrations are balanced you'll see rewards like new opportunities, dreams manifested and things changing for the better. However, if you are unbalanced, you'll feel a lot of tension and may have intense thoughts and emotional reactions.

HOW TO USE THIS ENERGY: Enjoy the gifts the moon has given to you, but don't run away with your emotions. Be open to new things and bask in the glow of your light.

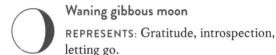

Waning gibbous moon

REPRESENTS: Gratitude, introspection, letting go.

WHAT IT DOES: Coming down from our high, we start feeling grateful for the abundance we have received. You might feel rich in emotions and want to share your joy with those around you. However, be careful who you give your energy to as energy vampires are always lurking.

HOW TO USE THIS ENERGY: While you are still radiating happiness and light, this is a great time to ditch bad habits and remove negative thinking from your life. Practise your communication skills by successfully cutting energy vampires out of your life while still being generous to those around you.

Third quarter moon

REPRESENTS: Banishment, self-reflection, forgiveness.

WHAT IT DOES: As the light from the moon begins to fade, it's time to release everything that has been hurting you. Reflect on what has caused you anger and sorrow and let it go – it was holding you back from your higher purpose.

HOW TO USE THIS ENERGY: Forgive people, even if they haven't asked for forgiveness. Forgive yourself for the mistakes you made in the past – you are a different person now. Release your grudges.

Waning crescent moon

REPRESENTS: Balance, wisdom, rest.

WHAT IT DOES: Right before the moon loses the rest of its light, we still have one sliver left. During this phase, we may feel empty and drained, but really we are preparing our bodies and minds for the next cycle of learning and healing. We cannot stop the tides from rolling in, nor can we stop the moon from changing. All we can do is let the waves crash over us and accept it.

HOW TO USE THIS ENERGY: Relax and reflect on everything you have learned during this cycle by writing it down in a journal. Meditate and take care of your spiritual needs.

> **TIP:** Figure out the phase of the moon when you were born (you can look it up online), as it can tell you a lot about your mood, energy and personality. For example, if you were born under a full moon you may be more intense than someone who was born under a waning crescent moon.

Remember that, like the moon, you are always transitioning through different phases of your life. If you aren't happy in the current phase, don't lose hope because another cycle is coming. Honour the current phase, take the knowledge it has given you and move on to the next.

❧ HERBAL HEALING ❧

Long before traditional Western medicine and technology, humans were using the plants provided by the earth to heal the mind, body and soul of a person. Herbal healing, also known as herbalism, has been around since 3000 BC and has been used by almost every culture on the planet: from the indigenous people of North America who believe plants possess their own spirit, to African tribes who use herbs for purification during ritual ceremonies. The belief that certain herbs have the ability to open and unblock particular chakras originated in ancient India; while Chinese herbology is based on the concepts of yin, yang and qi energy, where the herbs can either cool (yin) or stimulate (yang) certain parts of the body.

Today, herbalism has become popular again as people seek alternative methods of healing. Modern witches also use herbs for spell work.

While certain herbs can work wonders on physical pains like stomach upsets and skin issues, they can also help heal your spirit, get rid of energy blocks and boost your vibrations overall. When your spirit is healthy, your body is healthy.

In this section we will be discussing different ways to incorporate herbal healing into our lives, as well as discovering what type of herbs will be most beneficial to our overall healing.

NOTE: Please remember to use herbal healing as a supplement to any medicine you are already using, NOT as a replacement for treatment from a medical professional. Please do extensive research before putting anything in or on your body, especially if you have allergies or sensitive skin. Please talk to your doctor before using herbs on a regular basis, or if you are pregnant or breastfeeding. Be safe!

Ways to use herbal healing

The beauty of herbs is that they are so versatile and there are so many different ways to get the full benefit of their powers – from consuming them in food and drink to making them into candles. Here are just a few ways to incorporate herbal healing in your daily life.

Essential oils

As mentioned in Chapter Two, essential oils are compounds extracted from plants that capture their scent and "essence", and are important things to have in your spiritual toolkit. Essential oils are an excellent way to use plants in your spiritual healing, especially if you cannot get hold of the plants themselves. You can put a few drops of an essential oil into a diffuser and practise aromatherapy, rub diluted essential oil on the pulse points of your skin, use the oil to make a candle to light during your healing or use lotion and balms with essential oils and massage them into your skin.

Smoke cleanse

A smoke cleanse is the process of burning a herb, incense stick, wood – or anything that is safe to burn and has cleansing properties – and using the smoke to cleanse a certain area or object. Use a smoke cleanse to clean the negative vibes from a room and your tools before you start your spiritual work. Please make sure you practise good fire safety while doing a smoke cleanse – burning down your home does not produce good vibes.

Tea

If you enjoy a nice cup of tea at night to relax or put the kettle on when feeling under the weather, then herbal healing is for you. One of the easiest ways to get the full benefits of your plants is by brewing them in a tea. There are many different herbal teas you can buy or you can make your own. You can also put herbs into drinks like lattes and other coffees.

Food

Another simple way to get the benefits of herbal healing is to eat the herbs (if they are edible, of course). Cook food with the herbs you want to enjoy the benefits of or bake them in a tasty dessert.

Gardening

Many herbs that carry spiritual benefits do not need to be bought, they can be grown in your own garden. Even if you don't have much space in your home, you can have a windowsill garden where you can watch your herbs grow and thrive. As you tend to your herbs, imagine you're attending to your spiritual energy. The more you take care of it and the more your plants grow, the more your spirit is being nurtured.

Herbs for spiritual healing

There are many herbs in the world and each carries a spiritual as well as a medical benefit. Here are a few of the more common herbs that can help you on your healing journey.

Lavender

Beautiful to look at and lovely to smell, lavender is essential in every herbalism toolkit. Native to the Mediterranean, the Middle East and India, the history of this flowering plant dates back over 2,500 years. Pagan witches used to throw lavender in their midsummer fires as a sacrifice to the ancient gods as lavender was considered a holy herb.

GOOD FOR: Cleansing energies, physical and emotional healing, longevity, increasing intelligence, communicating with spirits, clarity and psychic visions, stress relief, relieving anxiety, depression, insomnia and restlessness.

BEST USED IN: Essential oils, aromatherapy, teas, candles, smoke cleanse, placing it in a pillow and sleeping with it, even taking a bath with it.

Rosemary

Used in many dishes, rosemary is a store-cupboard staple. Native to the Mediterranean, this herb has been around for centuries and has been used for spiritual healing by the ancient Greeks, Christians, pagan witches and more.

GOOD FOR: Spiritual blessings, protection from negative vibrations and people, attracting love, healing and purification.

BEST USED IN: Smoke cleanse, cooking.

Camomile

Everyone's favourite sleepy-time tea, camomile does a lot to help stimulate good vibes just as much as it helps to put your mind at ease and your body at rest. Camomile, also known as manzanilla, has been documented as being used as far back as ancient Egypt.

GOOD FOR: Banishing negative vibrations, preventing nightmares, attracting love, stress relief, soothing anxiety and lowering heart rate.

BEST USED IN: Teas, lotions, essential oils.

Mint

Mint is popular in food and beverages for its fresh and zingy taste, but it can also bring many spiritual benefits. In ancient Egypt, mint was used to treat diseases and menstrual pains.

GOOD FOR: Purification, protection, boosting energy, communication, vitality, warding off negativity, encouraging good spirits, improving focus and reducing stress.

BEST USED IN: Teas and other drinks, aromatherapy, essential oils, massage oil.

Jasmine

Jasmine is highly important and powerful when it comes to spiritual work. Delicate and dainty, with a lovely floral scent, jasmine can pack a punch if used correctly.

GOOD FOR: Creating good vibrations, nurturing happiness, increasing psychic awareness, improving sleep, protection, increasing mental alertness, treating anxiety and depression.

BEST USED IN: Teas, candles, lotions, essential-oil perfumes, aromatherapy and soaps.

Star anise

Also known as anis estrella, star anise looks beautiful and smells wonderful, too. Star anise is the fruit of the Chinese *Illicium verum* tree and has been used in traditional Chinese herbalism for centuries. It tastes like liquorice. Either add ground star anise or cook with it whole to impart flavour and then remove before serving.

GOOD FOR: Productive calm, protection from energy vampires and bad vibes, increasing psychic awareness and boosting the immune system.

BEST USED IN: Food, incense, soap, candles, tea.

Aloe vera

You will no doubt already know of this plant's ability to heal sunburn and soothe dry skin, but you probably didn't know that it can be a balm for your spiritual burns as well. This plant has been used in medicine and spiritual healing for many years, and it looks great around the house.

GOOD FOR: Attracting good vibrations, relieving loneliness, attracting love, stimulating spirituality and banishing negativity.

BEST USED IN: Lotions, face creams, mists.

Dandelion

Don't break out the weedkiller just yet – dandelions are actually really good for you when it comes to spiritual healing, even if you don't think they make your lawn look pretty. Before they were labelled weeds, dandelions were used in ancient herbalism to heal illnesses. Easy to find and hard to kill, you can collect these little flowers with ease.

GOOD FOR: Increasing spirituality and emotional strength, increasing survival instincts, promoting adaptability and communicating with spirits.

BEST USED IN: Tea, wine, food, candles.

☸ CHROMOTHERAPY ☸

Has putting on a certain colour of clothing helped you feel more confident in yourself? Have you ever avoided wearing certain colours because they just don't feel right? If you said "yes" to these questions, then you've already experienced the powers and influence that colour can have on you.

We all know that colour has symbolic meanings in various cultures – a bride wears white on her wedding day, mourners wear black at a funeral – but colour also carries its own form of energy vibration and spiritual meaning. When you use a certain colour you are using its energy to manifest something into your life – whether it's to soothe your soul or improve your mood.

Chromotherapy, or colour healing, is the practice of using hues and lights for therapeutic purposes in an effort to improve a person's mood and mental health. By using colour, we can adjust our body's vibrations by working on certain energy points to rebalance us and bring in harmony.

How does chromotherapy work?

Colours are a visible spectrum seen through our eyes due to the particular wavelength of electromagnetic reflection bouncing off objects. This light is broken down into seven rays, with various shading differences based on their frequency and our eye's perception. Everything in this world is a combination of different colours and each has their own energy, including the organs and atoms in our body. Each particular colour can influence the flow and energy through us. When all the colours join together it results in white light, which brings completeness and union to all parts of the body.

We cannot see colour without light and we need light – especially the sun's light – to thrive. Without enough of it, some people fall into a deep depression during the winter when the sunlight is at its minimum, known as seasonal affective disorder or SAD.

On a psychological level, colour affects our perceptions. Painting a room in light colours makes the space look bigger; eating from a blue plate makes you less likely to overeat; and when we see red, we usually take it as a warning of danger. Colour also affects our perceptions of the world and ourselves on both an individual and a cultural level.

Some people gravitate toward certain colours and shy away from others. That's why asking, "What's your favourite colour?" isn't a silly question; it gives us a glimpse into what someone likes in themselves and what they value.

Every colour has meaning and those meanings give us messages that we must learn to read. So, if you start seeing a certain colour frequently or start gravitating toward items in a certain hue, it can be your subconscious' way of trying to give you the balance and healing you need.

You can perform chromotherapy by doing light therapy, carrying around crystals or wearing clothes in your chosen colour.

History

Chromotherapy began in ancient Egypt, where people used colour for healing purposes. According to Egyptian mythology, chromotherapy was created by Thoth, the god of writing and wisdom. The Egyptians and the ancient Greeks used colour crystals and dyes as treatment for certain ailments and sanctuaries were painted in various shades to stimulate healing.

In ancient India, the chakra system (see page 57) comprises the seven focal points of the body and each is associated with a specific colour that represents what the chakra does in the body. If a certain chakra is blocked, apply the colour associated with that chakra on to the body to realign it.

While chromotherapy today is not recommended as a treatment for illnesses, people are embracing colour healing and the positive influence that colour has on our moods and well-being. Try using light therapy to improve your mood, lift feelings of depression and give you an energy boost.

Auras

Have you ever met someone that you associate with a certain colour? They might not wear that colour a lot, but when you think of them you just see that colour palette? If yes, then you may have been reading their aura.

The aura is an electromagnetic energy field composed of wavelengths that surrounds the body. It is a spiritual energy that cannot be seen by the human eye, but can be felt intuitively. Each aura is made up of seven layers that correlate with different parts of your mental, physical, emotional and spiritual well-being. Everyone's aura is predominantly one colour and that colour – and how strong the colour is – provides insight into your spiritual health. Those who have strong, clean-coloured auras give off good vibrations and people want to be around them; while those with murky-coloured auras tend to give off bad vibes and are not that much fun to be around. If our auras are healthy, we are healthy.

What colour is my aura?

This can be difficult to answer because we can't *see* our auras. However, there are a few ways to find out. One way is getting your aura read by a professional who can tap into your energy and tell you the colour, shade and textures of your aura, and explain their meaning to you. Another method is to have your aura photographed. Aura photographing involves sitting to have your photo taken with a Polaroid-like camera that captures your aura by using double exposure and sensors that are attached to the chair. These sensors are laced with silver, which can easily pick up on your energies, so when the picture is taken it can capture your aura.

However, if you cannot find an aura reader or photographer near you, you can also see your aura yourself by using visualization and meditating on your aura colour (although this can take months or even years to discover). By learning the colour of your aura, you can use chromotherapy to keep it balanced.

Colour meaning and benefits

We have talked a lot about colours, but what do they represent? And what colour should you be using for your own spiritual healing? Here is a quick guide to each colour, what they mean and how they can benefit you.

Red

REPRESENTS: Passion, courage, strength, inspiration and ambition.

HEALING PROPERTIES: Known as the "great energizer", red gives us a boost when we are feeling low, helping with fatigue and invigorating people with red's ambition and drive. People who feel unstable and are searching for foundation can find comfort with red's grounding energies.

Red is also a great pain reliever as it releases tension from the muscles as well as the tension in our souls. Red gives us the strength to fight another day.

AURA: You are a dominating personality who is naturally drawn to leadership positions. You are passionate, driven, courageous and constantly seeking adventure. You may have an aggressive or stubborn side.

Orange

REPRESENTS: Sensuality, creativity, pride, optimism.

HEALING PROPERTIES: Orange brings out soothing, healing energies that warm the body and mind. It can relieve feelings of repression and gives us hope that things will get better. This colour stimulates creative thinking and breaks through writer's block with new ideas and enthusiasm.

AURA: Easy-going by nature, you have a warm, friendly way about you that people are drawn to. You have a magnetic sex appeal.

Yellow

REPRESENTS: Happiness, self-esteem, friendliness, knowledge.

HEALING PROPERTIES: The colour of learning, yellow is great for those who need inspiration or help absorbing information. Yellow alleviates our nervousness and keeps us energized as we become more aware of the world around us. Yellow is great for those suffering from burnout.

AURA: You have a lust for life and a keen intellect that gets you noticed. You are constantly busy with your many projects, but manage to stay cheerful and optimistic. You believe in yourself and people trust you easily.

Green

REPRESENTS: Hope, intuition, healing, prosperity.

HEALING PROPERTIES: Known as the universal healer, green gives the "okay" to go and heal anything, both in the body and the mind. You can use green for any type of spiritual healing you may need, but it works best in creating harmony, finding clarity and inner peace and encouraging forgiveness.

AURA: You are the "parent" in your friend group as you are always taking care of those around you. You feel at peace when you are out in nature and love being outdoors. You have a healing energy that many flock to.

Blue

REPRESENTS: Harmony, communication, wisdom, devotion.

HEALING PROPERTIES: The anti-stress colour of the rainbow, blue is instantly calming, easing our anxieties and relaxing the body so the mind can get to sleep without nightmares or nagging thoughts. Blue also improves how we communicate with others and can help break bad patterns as well as aid in addiction recovery.

AURA: You are popular and well-liked by everyone you meet. You have many creative talents.

Indigo

REPRESENTS: Spirituality, idealism, mystery, intuition.

HEALING PROPERTIES: Indigo is one of the most mentally stimulating colours in the spectrum, enhancing our imagination and creative talents, and helping us visualize what we wish to manifest in life. It also clears our energy, purifying the murkier parts of our auras, and brings us pleasant dreams. Above all, indigo connects us with our spirituality.

AURA: You can feel other people's energies as easily as you feel your own. You are introverted and difficult to get to know, but fearless, and deeply intuitive.

Violet

REPRESENTS: Power, wisdom, compassion, psychic energy.

HEALING PROPERTIES: Violet has the power to transform your life. It heals melancholy and addiction, and soothes emotional distress while you detox. Violet slows you down to make you realize what you need to do in order to heal. It unlocks your spiritual insight, allowing you to be reborn again.

AURA: People are intimidated by you because you have a higher vibration than most. Creative and intuitive, you just want to make the world a better place.

🪷 CHAKRA HEALING 🪷

If you've ever had any interest in New Age healing or metaphysics, or even simply taken a yoga class, then you've probably heard the term "chakra" before. But what exactly is a chakra?

Chakras are various focal points used in healing and meditation practices that seek to balance the mind, body and spirit in order for it to reach its maximum potential. Some view chakras as doorways to our spiritual power and the key to our ultimate enlightenment. Each chakra corresponds to a specific bundle of nerves, a major organ and a location on both our spiritual and physical body, each of which affects our overall well-being.

The word *chakra* comes from the Sanskrit word meaning "wheel" and this may be the best way to think about chakras: spinning wheels of energy, also known as prana, that have to stay open and align to their assigned area of the body. When all of our chakras are opened, prana can move freely throughout the body, ensuring the physical body, mind and spirit are in perfect harmony.

History of chakras

The idea and practice of chakra healing has been around for thousands of years, originating in ancient India. This system was first mentioned in the Vedas, the sacred scriptures of Hinduism, which date from 1500 to 1000 BC. The Vedas are written in Sanskrit, the ancient language of India, and are the foundation of Ayurvedic medicine and Hindu teachings. It is believed that each chakra contains a key to unlock the solution to our challenges and dilemmas – that they hold the secrets only our ancestors knew. With each solution unlocked, we can achieve full enlightenment. They also connect our physical body to our aura and energy fields.

The chakra system has fascinated spiritual practitioners for years and is still popular today as more and more people are trying to connect with their body and spirit, in an attempt to reach their highest purpose and heal their bodies and minds.

There are said to be around 114 chakras in the human body, but we'll only focus on the seven main chakras that run along the spine, from the base (the root chakra) to the top (the crown chakra) of the spine. Each of these main chakras has a corresponding name, colour, area of the spine and health focus.

A good chakra is an open chakra

When a chakra is open, that energy is flowing throughout our body with ease and we are experiencing the benefits of that chakra at full power. However, when a chakra is blocked, no new energy can go through it, leaving only the negative energy. But how does a chakra get blocked?

When our energies become negative and our vibrations turn toward the dark side, our chakras can become closed off from positive energies. Negative energy can come from a variety of places: self-limiting beliefs, unhealed trauma, unresolved anger and resentment, stress, exhaustion, poor lifestyle choices, not taking care of your physical and spiritual body, and external sources.

However, activities like yoga, breathing exercises, visualization, meditation and repeating mantras can all help up to reopen our chakras.

A brief introduction to each chakra

You know what chakras are, but what are the main chakras? As mentioned previously, each of the seven main chakras have their own area of focus as well as control of certain organs and emotions, and there are different ways to open them up. They each also have a related location (or locations) on the physical body – for instance, if you have knee pain your root chakra could be blocked. If you want to open that chakra, it's good to work with those parts of the body to heal it. For example, if you have issues with your root chakra, walking outside barefoot could help because this chakra is about being connected to the ground. We'll spend the next few pages going over each one, giving you a brief guide.

Root chakra (Muladhara)

LOCATION: Base of spine.

COLOUR: Red.

REPRESENTS: Survival, security, self-preservation, the physical body.

RELATED AREAS OF THE BODY: Feet, knees, legs, kidneys, adrenals, large intestines, base of spine.

ISSUES IF BLOCKED: Low self-esteem, insecurities about needs being met, co-dependency.

HOW TO OPEN: Mindful walking/jogging, dancing, standing meditation, showering.

Sacral chakra (Svadhisthana)

LOCATION: Lower abdomen.

COLOUR: Orange.

REPRESENTS: Sexuality, pleasure, creativity, relationships, sensual desires and connections.

RELATED AREAS OF THE BODY: Reproductive organs, urinary system, spleen, lower back.

ISSUES IF BLOCKED: Guilt, depression, low self-esteem, insecurity, detachment, fear.

HOW TO OPEN: Yoga, belly dancing, building healthy relationships.

Solar plexus chakra (Manipura)

LOCATION: Base of ribcage.

COLOUR: Yellow.

REPRESENTS: Our willpower, control, identity, ego.

RELATED AREAS OF THE BODY: Digestive system, liver, gall bladder.

ISSUES IF BLOCKED: Shame, addictive tendencies, inability to set boundaries with others, co-dependency, lack of self-control, depression, anxiety.

HOW TO OPEN: Meditation, deep breathing.

Heart chakra (Anahata)

LOCATION: Heart.

COLOUR: Green.

REPRESENTS: Love, compassion, harmony, forgiveness, empathy.

RELATED AREAS OF THE BODY: Heart, lungs, circulatory system, arms, hands.

ISSUES IF BLOCKED: Grief, over-sensitivity, defensiveness, martyr complex, isolation, lack of forgiveness.

HOW TO OPEN: Being in nature, healthy relationship with family members, self-care, forgiveness.

Throat chakra (Vishuddha)

LOCATION: Throat.

COLOUR: Blue.

REPRESENTS: Communication, truth, creativity, self-expression.

RELATED AREAS OF THE BODY: Throat, ears, mouth, shoulders, neck.

ISSUES IF BLOCKED: Inability to tell the truth, manipulation, arrogance, anxiety, low self-esteem, compulsive eating.

HOW TO OPEN: Singing, chanting, breathing exercises, aromatherapy.

Brow chakra (third eye) (Ajna)

LOCATION: Forehead.

COLOUR: Indigo.

REPRESENTS: Insight, intuition, harmony, imagination.

RELATED AREAS OF THE BODY: Eyes, base of skull, brow.

ISSUES WHEN BLOCKED: Hallucinations, mental fog, feeling overwhelmed, paranoia, being judgmental.

HOW TO OPEN: Meditation, visualization, aromatherapy.

Crown chakra (Sahasrara)

LOCATION: Top of head.

COLOUR: Violet.

REPRESENTS: Higher power, spirituality, understanding.

RELATED AREAS OF THE BODY: Central nervous system, cerebral cortex, pineal gland.

ISSUES WHEN BLOCKED: Loneliness, lack of direction, inability to achieve goals, feeling disconnected spiritually, feeling lost, insomnia, depression.

HOW TO OPEN: Meditation, yoga.

Keep these chakras in mind as you move throughout this book as they are an important part of healing, and many of the practices mentioned ahead will be focused on opening, unblocking and healing your chakras.

🪷 REIKI HEALING 🪷

Reiki is a Japanese energy-healing technique designed to rebalance and realign the body's natural flow of energy, or *ki* in Japanese. During a reiki session, the practitioner places their hands either directly on or just above the patient to stimulate the natural healing abilities in the patient's body. Reiki healers can also identify any energy blocks a patient may have in their chakras and remove them. While reiki does not cure diseases, it can be used to manage symptoms, reduce stress, promote relaxation and heal the mind and spirit.

Reiki is non-intrusive and can be incredibly relaxing, which is one of the reasons this healing practice has become so popular in recent years.

History of reiki

The word "reiki" is made up of two Japanese words: *rei*, which means "God's wisdom", and *ki*, which means "life-force energy". Putting it all together, reiki translates as "spiritually guided life-force energy".

Unlike many of the other healing practices mentioned in this book, reiki is relatively modern. It was developed in the 1920s by Dr Mikao Usui in Japan. Throughout his life, Usui had an avid interest in medicine, psychology and theology, performing different forms of medicine and spiritual practices in the hopes of healing himself and others. Despite being a spiritual man, he wanted to find a non-religious form of healing that could be accessible to everyone. During his life, he travelled the whole world before becoming a Buddhist monk and living in a monastery, which is where he developed the reiki system.

It is said that reiki was developed when Usui had a spiritual awakening after spending 21 days fasting, meditating and praying in a cave on Mount Kurama in Kyoto. On the morning of the 21st day, Usui had a vision of ancient Sanskrit symbols (the chakras) that helped him develop the system that would use the laying of the hands to heal another. That day, reiki healing was born.

Usui went on to establish a reiki clinic for healing and teaching in Kyoto in 1922, but he wasn't finished yet. Before his death in 1926, Usui developed reiki even further by adding hand positions that covered more of the body, and incorporated the "reiki ideals" to the practice to add spiritual balance.

The five reiki ideals include:

1 Do not anger.

2 Do not worry.

3 Be filled with gratitude.

4 Devote yourself to your work.

5 Be kind to others.

Usui believed that taking individual responsibility for your own spiritual healing and devoting yourself to self-improvement was the key to achieving a lasting result. Reiki healing can only take a person so far and the rest of the work is up to the patient.

After Usui's death, the students he taught would go on to heal each other and spread the practice throughout the world, and it is still popular today.

The reiki session

Reiki is a non-intrusive healing treatment that can be performed by a trained reiki professional. You can be taught to do reiki on yourself – weekend classes can get you started at a basic level to allow self-treatment. Reiki was created to be simple enough so that anyone can become a reiki master when given proper training.

So, what can you expect during your first appointment?

To start, your healer will explain a bit more about reiki and their process for healing. You'll also discuss your expectations and what you would like to focus on or heal: depression, anxiety, feeling stuck in a rut, healing from past traumas, etc. You can also let your healer know any particular areas where you have injuries or places you just don't want to be touched. Then, you will be asked to lie down on a table and will be covered with a blanket. The practitioner will move their hands around your body either lightly touching or moving their hands over you. Allow yourself to feel whatever emotions arise and let them go.

Healing benefits from reiki

There are many benefits to be gained from practising reiki healing, such as:

- Relieving symptoms of anxiety.
- Relieving emotional and spiritual fatigue.
- Alleviating some symptoms of depression.
- Boosting quality of life.
- Boosting mood.
- Helping with insomnia.
- Reducing stress.
- Promoting harmony within the body.
- Balancing vibrations.
- Releasing tension in the body.
- Improving focus.
- Cleansing your emotions.
- Activating the body's self-healing abilities.

... and much more.

What spiritual lessons can we learn from reiki?

More than just a tool for healing, reiki can also teach us spiritual lessons. By using and understanding reiki, we can learn to live more spiritually by growing to be more open to positive energy and new ideas and being more adaptable. Reiki also teaches us how negative self-talk and thinking can be harmful to our physical and spiritual body. We cannot always control what happens in our lives, but we can control our reactions to them. We can choose to be negative or we can choose to express gratitude and be optimistic toward life, believing that everything will turn out okay.

This is not an easy lesson to learn. In fact, it may take many years to unlearn negative self-talk. There will also be aspects of your life that are negative and not your fault – it's okay to feel anger and to be upset. The idea is to not live in your anger and misery, but to strive to make your world and the world around you a better place.

Hand placements for self-healing

As mentioned, you can learn to perform reiki on yourself after taking a short course. However, if you don't have any reiki classes in your area, or cannot wait until the next one, here are 12 key hand placements to practise self-healing at home. Before trying these placements, remember to meditate for a few moments to help you become completely grounded.

Start by holding your hand in these positions for a minute or two each. Once you get used to doing reiki on yourself you can try these hand placements for longer periods of time.

- **FIRST POSITION:** Place both palms on your face, cupping them lightly over your eyes with your fingers touching your forehead without any pressure.

- **SECOND POSITION:** Place your hands on both sides of your head with the heel of your hand resting near your ears and your fingertips touching the crown of your head.

- **THIRD POSITION:** Cross your arms behind your head with one hand on the back of your head while the other hand is above the nape of your neck.

- **FOURTH POSITION:** Place your chin inside the palm of your cupped hands as your hands are wrapped along the jawline, like you are holding your head in your hands.

- **FIFTH POSITION:** Hold your neck in one hand by using your thumb and fingers, forming a "V". Rest your other hand between your collarbone and heart.

- **SIXTH POSITION:** Place your hands on your upper ribcage with your elbows relaxed.

- **SEVENTH POSITION:** Move your hands down to your stomach, resting them above the navel and allowing the fingertips to touch.

- **EIGHTH POSITION:** Place one hand over each side of the pelvic bone and allow the tips of your fingers to touch.

- **NINTH POSITION:** Reach your arms over your head and place them on your shoulder blades, bending your elbows.

- **TENTH POSITION:** Reach behind your back and place your hands on the centre of your spine, bending your elbows.

- **ELEVENTH POSITION:** Slide your hands down to the lower part of your back.

- **TWELFTH POSITION:** Lower your arms and cup your hands on your tail bone.

Try these hand positions whenever you are having a stressful day or when your vibrations feel off. If you have limited mobility in terms of where your hands can reach, just move where you can. This is a guide that is easily adaptable, not written in stone.

🪷 AYURVEDA 🪷

Ayurveda is one of the oldest systems of holistic healing in the world, and is based on the belief that wellness depends on the balance between the body, mind and spirit. All life, according to Ayurveda, must be supported by well-balanced energy. When our energy is balanced, we are in our best health and best frame of mind. When we are unbalanced, our health and spirit become drained, making us prone to illness and negative self-talk, which affect our overall quality of life.

Practitioners of Ayurveda believe that every person is made up of the five basic elements: space (or the ether), air, fire, water and earth, combined with the three life forces of energies called doshas. Each dosha has control of a different bodily function and they all come together to keep the body working in harmony. While everyone has a unique combination of the three, there is usually one that is stronger than the rest, which gives some insight into our personality and moods.

Ayurveda puts more emphasis on the prevention of illness and maintaining a healthy balance of energies through the use of herbs, special massages, positive thoughts and overall lifestyle changes. Ayurveda isn't meant to cure any diseases or illness, and is often used alongside Western medicine or surgery in order to help the body and rebalance your energies.

History of Ayurveda

Ayurveda has been around for thousands of years, although the exact timeline of the practice is unclear. Many believe that it could be as old as 6,000 years, while others think it is more recent, going back only 3,000 years. We do know that Ayurveda comes from the Vedic culture in India. Ayurveda in Sanskrit translates to "the science of life".

Part of the reason that Ayurveda's timeline is foggy is because it was passed down for hundreds of years strictly through the oral tradition, as one master would teach the principles of natural healings to their students who would go on to treat others. In fact, books about Ayurveda were not written until the eighth century BC. What we know about Ayurveda today comes from the *Brhat Trayi* ("the great triad"), which consists of three important texts: *Charaka Samhita*, *Sushruta Samhita* and *Ashtanga Hridayam Samhita*. These texts give the basic principles of Ayurveda, which became the modern Ayurveda we know today. However, because the practice was taught orally, there are many theories and practices that originally came from Ayurveda that are now simply lost to the ages.

The practice of Ayurveda has nearly died out many times throughout history, when India was occupied by various countries, which almost destroyed India's culture, religion and literature.

However, Ayurveda was revived in the twentieth century when India achieved independence, which brought about a renewed focus on restoring its cultural practices. Today, Ayurveda is widely practised in India as a means of alternative medicine and has spread to other countries as well.

The three doshas

Ayurveda teaches that there are three principal energies in the body called doshas. They are believed to flow through the body and keep your energies balanced. Each dosha has a certain job to do and many things are related to and affected by it, such as personality, mood and temperament. Doshas are also associated with certain elements.

Vata dosha

 Vata dosha, or vata for short, is energy of movement and is believed to be the most powerful of all three doshas. It deals with the essential bodily motions such as cell division, blood flow and the pumping of your heart, and gets rid of waste through your intestinal system. Basically, we would die without vata accounting to Ayurveda. We wouldn't even exist.

Vata is composed of the elements space (ether) and air. It also governs all movement in the body, both voluntary and involuntary, such as breathing, blinking and muscle movements. Vata also represents the qualities of quick wit and intellect, flexibility and creativity. People whose dominant dosha is vata are often very smart and able to understand a lot of information in a short amount of time. They are very active and move quickly.

Personality-wise, people who are vata-dominant are strong-willed, bold, confident and can easily adapt to new situations. On the other hand, they are also very forgetful, restless and not great at planning ahead.

When vata is out of balance, a person may feel fearful and nervous, and have trouble paying attention for long periods of time. They may also experience lapses in memory. Money is quickly spent and not well managed. Since vata is ruled by space and wind, it's difficult to stay grounded.

One way to balance your vata is by creating a routine for yourself: waking up at the same time every day, eating at a scheduled time, working out and going to bed at a reasonable hour. It is also good to avoid cold weather and seek warm climates, colours or foods.

Pitta

 Pitta rules over the body's metabolism, absorption, nutrition, digestion and temperature. Pitta is composed of fire and water, so those who are pitta-dominant tend to be more hot-headed than others. In balance, pitta promotes our intelligence and understanding of others. When out of balance, we become angry and jealous.

People who are pitta-dominant have very sharp minds and are highly intellectual, making excellent leaders and planners. They have strong appetites for everything: food, power, money. They like to have a lot of possessions and enjoy showing them off to others. However, pitta people also have a very short temper. It's easy to get on their nerves and invoke their jealous side.

When the pitta is unbalanced in the body, they may be quick to become angry, with even minor things causing great annoyance. They may become overly critical and pessimistic. Nothing is ever quite good enough. Physically, this can manifest in skin irritation, nervous sweating, fever and diarrhoea.

Some ways to balance out your pitta include avoiding getting overheated, eating non-spicy foods and exercising only when it's cool. Stick to cooler weather, colours and food.

Kapha

 Last, but certainly not least, the third dosha is kapha, the energy of structure. Kapha is the glue that holds the cells in the body together. Made up of earth and water, it supplies the water and fluids for all the bodily systems. It lubricates the joints, moisturizes the skin and helps the immune system. It also controls muscle growth and strength. In balance, kapha gives us feelings of love, calmness, stamina and the ability to forgive others. Out of balance, we could experience co-dependency, greed and envy of others.

Kapha-dominant people have calm personalities. They are tolerant and quick to forgive. They have excellent long-term memories even if it takes them a few minutes to "get" certain concepts. They move slowly but get pretty far. Kapha people prefer stability and are generally grounded. They save money easily. However, they can be pretty sluggish and stay set in their ways, and they can also be overly possessive and greedy.

When the kapha is unbalanced, a person can become stuck in their lives, unable to move forward or make changes. They may fall into co-dependent relationships that are difficult to leave. They become afraid of change, preferring the devil that you know. Mentally, kapha imbalances manifest themselves as feelings of lethargy, neediness and depression; while physically they can manifest themselves in headaches, nausea, poor appetite, high blood pressure and frequent colds.

One way to balance your kapha is by switching around your routine every so often to avoid falling into a rut. It's also a good idea to exercise regularly and avoid naps.

How to discover your dominant dosha

Our dosha type shows up in a variety of ways: our appearance, body frame, how we react under stress, and the type of foods and weathers we gravitate toward. When you figure out your dominant dosha, it is easier to treat the rest of your body.

Your dominant dosha may be vata if you...

- Are smaller than others in height and weight.
- Have a pale complexion or lighter skin.
- Forget to eat or do not have a strong appetite.
- Have dry skin.
- Have dry hair that breaks easily.
- Are a light sleeper.
- Are always cold.
- Like change and are enthusiastic toward nature.
- Become anxious under pressure.

Your dominant dosha may be pitta if you...

- Are of medium height.
- Gain and lose weight easily.
- Always feel warm.
- Have a high hairline and thin (possibly reddish) hair.
- Like to be in a leadership position.
- Have sensitive skin that's easily irritated.
- Have freckles or moles on your skin.
- Have an intense gaze.
- Are a moderately sound sleeper.
- Are ambitious and exacting.
- Become aggressive under pressure.

Your dominant dosha may be kapha if you...

- Are full-figured.

- Gain weight easily.

- Have thick, healthy hair, though a little oily.

- Have smooth, oily skin.

- Have large, kind eyes.

- Are a deep sleeper who has trouble waking up.

- Do not like cold, wet days.

- Are supportive and easy-going.

- Are reclusive under pressure.

Ways to practise Ayurveda

The idea of Ayurveda may feel overwhelming to some people if you don't know where to begin. Since Ayurveda is an ancient form of healing, there are many ways to incorporate it into your own spiritual healing and life. Here are some forms of Ayurvedic healing for you to try:

MEDITATION: Meditation is a wonderful way to calm your mind and rebalance the body by being still and making yourself more aware of your emotional state and intentions. Meditate before going to bed at night and before meals to practise mindful eating.

PRANYAMA (BREATHING EXERCISES): The best way to get positive energy flowing throughout the body is by taking deep breaths. Diaphragmatic breathing from deep in your belly increases the intake of oxygen, while also massaging your internal organs and stimulating your metabolism.

HERBALISM: Using herbs is an original part of Ayurvedic medicine as they can be used to treat imbalances in the body's energy field.

MASSAGE: Massage is a great way to increase the blood and energy flow throughout the entire body to rebalance the doshas and reduce stress. It's best to have a massage performed by a professional, especially someone who specializes in Ayurvedic healing. However, you can give yourself a massage, perhaps using warm sesame or coconut oil. Remember to pay special attention to your joints and move in a circular motion.

SWEDANA (SWEATING): Sweat the bad vibes out by going to a *swedana*, an Ayurvedic spa treatment that involves a full-body massage followed by sitting in a steam room to open up your pores. The skin is the body's largest organ and when heated it is believed to release toxins and impurities from the body. Remember to hydrate well afterwards.

You can try all of these, or you can stick to a favourite if you prefer. Just remember that there are many ways to practise Ayurveda, so if one doesn't immediately work for you, there are plenty of other methods to try.

⚜ MAGNETIC HEALING ⚜

Magnetic healing is a type of energy healing practice that uses a weak, static (unmoving) magnetic field for healing benefits. As we know, the human body is made up of energy that is constantly moving throughout the body, unless it is blocked in a certain area. We also generate our own energy fields, otherwise known as auras. Magnets can manipulate the energy inside of the body to keep it flowing naturally as well as clearing energy blocks. When our auras are clean and realigned, we can enjoy physical and spiritual wellness.

Magnetic healing has been practised from as far back as 1200 BC, when Chinese healers used magnetic material like lodestone (a naturally magnetized mineral) to balance the flow of qi. Other cultures such as the ancient Indians, Greeks and Egyptians were also fascinated by the effects that magnetic substances have on the human body. One of the most famous users of magnetic healers was Cleopatra, Queen of Egypt, who was said to sleep with a lodestone.

In the sixteenth century, the Swiss physician Paracelsus theorized that there was a link between the mind and the body through a life force that he named "Archeus", which was influenced by the forces found in magnets. Because of this, magnets could be used to treat illness and promote self-healing. Paracelsus treated many of his patients using lodestones.

Public interest in magnetic healing grew during the eighteenth century in Europe when carbon steel magnets became readily available. The physician Franz Anton Mesmer practised magnetic healing during this period and is credited with coining the term "animal magnetism" to describe the life force in all living beings (his name is also where we get the word "mesmerize" from). Mesmer suggested that the animal magnetism emitted from human hands could cure people in the same way as lodestones or magnets, because we are made of energy.

Some research has shown magnets to increase blood flow, improve flexibility, increase muscle strength and promote relaxation among patients.

Many healers use magnets to unblock chakras, clear our auras and give us a reset on our energies. Think of your body as a battery and magnetic healing as a charger. If you start feeling low, the magnetic field can give you a boost until you become one hundred per cent charged again.

The benefits of magnetic healing

There are many benefits to magnetic healing that come with unblocking and aligning your energies. Here are a few:

- Increases clarity, removing confusion and doubt from your mind.
- Removes negative vibrations and negative thoughts like anger, resentment, betrayal and self-limiting beliefs.
- Increases focus on your life, career and family matters.
- Strengthens the mind, body and spirit.
- Helps emotional imbalances like low self-esteem, addiction, depression and eating disorders.
- Improves communication, confidence and the ability to make decisions.

Ways to use magnetic healing

NOTE: Due to the nature of magnetic healing, with magnets being so close to your body, this method is not recommended for those who are pregnant or have any metal implants in their bodies (pacemakers, steel plates, spinal rods, etc.). As always, talk to your doctor and do your research before trying magnetic healing. Stay safe, stay healthy.

There are many ways to practise magnetic healing to boost your vibrations and clear your aura. Some you can practise by yourself and for others you can visit a specialist in magnetic healing. Here are a few examples:

Wearing magnets

One of the more popular ways to perform magnetic healing is to have the magnet touch your skin in the form of a magnetic bracelet or ring. This works because the magnet is touching your body, getting close to your energy points so that it can readjust your energy field and vibrations. Some people wear magnets as shoe insoles for balance at their root chakra, while others sleep on a special mattress pad with a magnet in it to reach all of their chakras. You can buy wearable magnets at any New Age shop or on the internet. However, it's important to remember to not wear your magnetic jewellery at all times, or to take it off only to slip into your magnetic bed. Too much magnetic energy can make you very sick – the opposite of what you're trying to do.

Place body magnets on your blocked chakra

Another method of magnetic healing involves placing a magnet on the chakra that you are having an issue with and moving it up and down three times, releasing the blocked emotion or negativity and allowing your energy to flow freely again. For example, say you were having trouble with your root chakra. Place your magnet in front of the base of your spine, or on your feet and legs, and move the magnet from side to side three times until you start to feel a warm tingle – that's your chakra opening up. You can also run a magnet up and down your whole body to cleanse all of your chakras.

TRADITIONAL CHINESE MEDICINE

Traditional Chinese medicine, also known as TCM, is one of the oldest forms of medicine. TCM is based on the concept that a vital life force called qi surges through the body at all times and is interconnected with nature. The ancient Chinese believed that a human being is a microcosm of a larger surrounding universe. When we are connected to our own qi and the qi around us, we feel healthy and balanced. However, when we have an alteration to our qi we become imbalanced, causing illness, disease or distress. To address this, one must find balance between the internal organs and the external elements: earth, fire, water, wood and metal.

In TCM, everybody is unique, therefore every qi is unique and treatment is tailored to the individual. The practitioner will work with their client one-on-one to help them find the best way to balance the healthy and unhealthy qi within the body. Not every aspect of TCM treatment will work for every person and TCM understands that.

TCM also understands that treatment must support the entire body, including the mind and spirit, and do things to keep your physical and spiritual body as healthy as possible, even if the disease is still present. So even if you have a chronic condition, you can still enjoy a very active, happy lifestyle.

TCM uses different forms of treatment to help you unblock your qi and unlock your potential to develop your unique gifts. Its wisdom is in understanding an individual's health needs and empowering them to unite the mind, body and spirit.

The four key principles

When learning TCM, there are four key things to keep in mind:

1 Every single thing in your body, from your little toe to your biggest emotions, are a necessary part of your wholeness and make up the unique complexity of who you are. If you are missing something, be it physically or emotionally, your qi will be sent off balance and the flow will be blocked.

2 You are connected to nature at all times, so TCM factors in the seasonal changes, your location and the time of day when practising healing. It also looks at your age, genetics and other health issues.

3 You are born with the natural ability to self-heal. No matter what happens to you in this life, no matter what you have gone through, or what you're going through, you are not broken. Sometimes it may be harder to access your points of healing and you may need some extra assistance.

4 Prevention is key. It's easier to stay healthy and happy when you do not suffer from major energy blocks or injury in the first place, so if you're healthy now try your best to stay that way. How can you achieve that? By listening to your body, of course. TCM teaches us how to interpret the body's own warning signs that let us know something is not right. That twinge of pain? The lack of energy? Don't ignore those signs.

Yin and yang

In TCM, yin and yang are two opposing forces existing in the body, living in balance. This symbiotic relationship shows that the universe exists together as a collection of connected but opposite elements. Yin represents qi that is material, dark, negative, solid, passive, cooling and feminine. Yang represents qi that is immaterial, light, expanding, ascending, warm, bright, active and masculine.

While yin and yang are opposites, they cannot exist without each other. In fact, when you look at the yin-and-yang symbol you see a little circle of yang in yin and a little circle of yin in yang. This represents the fact that in order to achieve true balance you need a little light with darkness, a little chaos to balance order. There is no day without night.

They are always moving. If yang starts growing, yin may slow down. This is why it's important to keep your yin and yang balanced. Too much of either can be unhealthy.

The five elements

The theory of the five elements or the five phases of transformation is deeply woven into Chinese culture: from medical practices, to martial arts, to Feng Shui. It's based on the idea that all natural phenomena can be categorized into five elemental groups: fire, earth, water, wood and metal. This includes the seasons, directions, climate, our internal organs, emotions, colours, taste, personal growth and so on. It goes back to the second principle of TCM: we are connected to nature and constantly interacting with it. The five elements give the framework to recognize where our imbalances are in our mind, body and spirit, and how everything must stay connected to achieve balance.

Along with the five elements there are also five key organs observed in TCM, each having a corresponding element, colour, emotion and a specific meaning in the organ system. It is believed that when we are feeling negative it means that one of our organs is off balance.

Here is a brief overview of the five elements and organs:

Wood

Wood represents new life, full of vitality and hope.

The organ associated with wood is the liver. In TCM, the liver is in charge of all the qi in the body, making sure it's regulated and flowing smoothly. The liver is easily affected by negative energy.

SEASON: Spring

COLOUR: Green

CLIMATE: Windy

DIRECTION: East

EMOTION: Anger

TASTE: Sour

SIGNS OF IMBALANCE: Feelings of disproportionate anger, bitterness, irritability, resentment, frustration, flying off the handle, headaches, dry and red eyes, dizziness.

Fire

Fire represents ascending energy.

The organ associated with this element is the heart. The heart longs to express itself and becomes stressed and blocked when we are unable to be creative or reach our desires.

SEASON: Summer

COLOUR: Red

CLIMATE: Hot

DIRECTION: South

EMOTION: Happiness

TASTE: Bitter

SIGNS OF IMBALANCE: Insomnia, excessive dreaming, poor long-term memory, lack of enthusiasm toward life, depression.

Earth

Earth represents stable energy in the body.

The organ associated with this element is the spleen. In TCM, the spleen oversees the digestive system and the energy that moves through it. Any stress can affect the digestive system and disrupt the spleen's qi.

SEASON: Late summer

COLOUR: Yellow

CLIMATE: Damp

DIRECTION: Centre

EMOTION: Worry

TASTE: Sweet

SIGNS OF IMBALANCE: Loss of appetite, hyper-fixation, anxiety, worry, dwelling.

Metal

In nature, metal is found under the earth's crust, hence this energy is more internalized as we look inward into our spirits.

The organ associated with this element is the lungs. In TCM, the lungs are considered very delicate and responsible for nourishing the cells by taking in oxygen. By breathing in and out, the lungs teach us to take in things, like wisdom, and let things go, like negative feelings.

SEASON: Autumn

COLOUR: White

CLIMATE: Dry

DIRECTION: West

EMOTION: Grief

TASTE: Pungent

SIGNS OF IMBALANCE: Fatigue, coughs, frequent colds, allergies, dry skin, excessive crying, grief, sense of loss, sadness, detachment.

Water

Water's qi does not flow like the other elements, rather, it is known for its stillness.

The organ associated with this element is the kidneys. In TCM, the kidneys store the qi in the body for all the other organs that need it. Because the kidneys are holding so much energy, they need rest and plenty of it. You could also be afraid of running out of qi, because if the kidneys lose theirs, it can hurt all the other organs.

SEASON: Winter

COLOUR: Black

CLIMATE: Cold

DIRECTION: North

EMOTION: Fear

TASTE: Salty

SIGNS OF IMBALANCE: Poor short-term memory, lower back pain, ringing in the ears, hearing loss, hair loss, fear, insecurity, self-isolation.

TCM practices

There are many ways to practise TCM to balance the body. Some of these we've already touched on (herbalism) and others we will be discussing in greater depth later on in this chapter (acupuncture and qigong). However, here are some key practices to keep in mind.

ACUPUNCTURE: Probably the best-recognized TCM practice in the West, acupuncture involves inserting needles into the skin in order to keep the balance between yin and yang, and promote the normal flow of qi.

MOXIBUSTION: A type of therapy that involves burning moxa, also known as mugwort root, to heal the body. Mugwort is burned near the skin to stimulate the flow of qi. NOTE: Do not practise moxibustion without the guidance of a trained practitioner and avoid if you have lung problems.

HERBALISM: Special herbs are often a key part of TCM and are used in many different ways: teas, ointments, powder, etc. (see pages 38–46 for more details).

CUPPING: Cupping is a type of massage where a practitioner places several open spheres or "cups" on different parts of the body. Practitioners warm the cups first before placing them on the skin, then when the air cools the cups create a vacuum and stick to the skin.

TUI NA MASSAGE: A form of bodywork therapy that blends massage and acupressure together to unblock qi. Usually performed by a trained practitioner.

QIGONG: A system of coordinated body movements and meditation that focuses on balancing the body's qi, to benefit the body, mind and spirit.

🪷 QIGONG 🪷

Qigong combines slow sequences of movements with breathing exercises, as well as positive visualizations, to promote energy balances, good vibrations and positive thoughts. By getting the body moving, our energy is mobilized and more energy is created. By thinking positive thoughts and visualizing positivity into our lives, we are creating good energy and boosting our mood.

Qigong has been practised by millions of people around the world, but its roots stem from ancient Chinese culture. The word "qigong" is derived from two words: *qi*, meaning "vital life force", and *gong*, which means "work" or "cultivation". Putting that together, qigong roughly translates to "life-energy cultivation".

Qigong dates back over 4,000 years and there is a wide variety of forms, depending on the different regions of China and cultural practices where each type originated. In traditional Chinese medicine, qigong is used as a form of healing.

In Confucianism, qigong promotes longevity and is used to improve a person's moral character. In Daoism and Buddhism, qigong is performed as part of meditative practices. It is also used in Chinese martial arts to improve fighting ability. Traditionally, qigong is taught by a master to their students through training and oral history, so each qigong master may have their own particular style or focus.

In the 1940s and 1950s the Chinese government tried to integrate different forms of qigong into one coherent system of practice, but many versions of qigong still exist today and are practised by thousands of people around the world.

Qigong has many health benefits and, by studying this practice, you can manipulate the qi to promote self-healing and stress management.

Types of qigong

Qigong can be as simple or as complex as you want it to be and the individual can add many different elements to their practice. However, there are a few types of qigong that you might want to look into.

Martial qigong

Since qigong is a physical activity involving movement and balance, it makes sense that it can be used to improve an individual's performance in sports, from enhanced accuracy in tennis to better stamina in swimming. Martial qigong has extra emphasis on power, speed and stamina as it is more physical, focusing on the movements of the body rather than the visualization aspects. This practice can improve a person's flexibility, balance and coordination, as well as prevent injury.

Medical qigong

Medical qigong combines the use of breath work, physical movements, and mental visualization and intention in order to correct electromagnetic imbalances in the body, strengthen the body, regulate the nervous and immune systems and relieve pain. It is also believed that medical qigong can release deep-seated emotions that have been trapped in the body, as well as relieve stress.

Many hospitals, rehabilitation centres and physical therapists have used qigong therapy along with medical treatment on all types of patients, from those recovering from a major injury or surgery, to those undergoing chemotherapy treatments. The idea is that by moving the body you are working the muscles, generating positive vibrations and creating energy. When you are controlling your breathing, you are relaxing and calming the body. When you are visualizing a healthier, happier version of yourself, you are manifesting your visions into reality.

Spiritual qigong

This practice of qigong is less physical and more focused on the meditation aspect, paying more attention to the stillness of the body than actually moving it. Spiritual qigong increases a person's self-awareness and feeling of peace and harmony, especially if they are practising in nature. This part of qigong came from the Daoist and Buddhist aspect of the practice, but you do not have to be religious to try it.

You can find a special qigong master to teach you any one of these forms of qigong, or you can practise on your own by watching videos on the internet, or buying DVDs or books on the subject.

The three principles of qigong

No matter what form you practise or what you hope to gain from practising this type of healing, qigong allows you an opportunity to reconnect with your spirit. As you begin your qigong practice, keep these three simple principles in mind and apply them while you're learning:

- Correct your posture.
- Deepen your breathing.
- Open your mind.

You can also use these three simple principles throughout your day when you find yourself overwhelmed, stressed out or disconnected from your body. Just by carrying out these simple steps, you are putting this centuries-old practice to good use.

The benefits of qigong

There are many benefits that practising qigong can have on your spiritual healing. Here are just a few:

- Learning the power of positive thinking.
- Learning to manifest through visualization.
- Stress relief.
- Increasing focus and mental clarity.
- Improving self-awareness.
- Balancing your energies.
- Removing energy blocks.
- Improving balance.
- Developing discipline.
- Building willpower.
- Increasing concentration.

... and many others. Qigong is a great way to move your body and improve your spiritual health as well. Just a few minutes of practice each day can lead to big changes later on.

Practice moves

If you are interested in practising qigong, it's best to do it with a professional instructor. But here are a few moves to get you started.

Awakening the qi

Stand in a relaxed pose. Stretch your hands out in front of you, keeping them above your pelvis. Slowly, raise your arms up until they get to your shoulders. Then, move your hands until your palms are facing outward (as if you are about to wave to someone) and slowly let your arms drop down to where they were. Continue this for about five minutes.

Mabu (horse stance)

Stand with your back straight and your feet a step apart. Lower your hips to knee level, keeping your knees bent at a 90-degree angle. Then, turn your feet outward to about 45 degrees. Keep looking forward and stretch your hands out in front of you. Bend your elbows, bringing them behind your shoulders, so your hands (in fists, if you like) are held tightly either side of the base of your ribcage. Stay like this for 20 seconds.

ACUPUNCTURE AND ACUPRESSURE

Acupuncture is a form of treatment that involves the insertion of fine needles into your skin at strategic points of the body to treat pain, manage stress and improve your overall wellness. For those afraid of needles, the thought of sticking them into your body can be pretty disturbing, but the procedure is minimally invasive. Each acupuncture needle produces a tiny injury to the body that is small enough not to hurt, but lets the body know that it needs to respond.

Acupuncture dates back to at least 100 BC and hails from traditional Chinese medicine, which as we know was used to balance the flow of qi through the body's meridians (pathways). Traditional Chinese medicine asserts that the body is criss-crossed by invisible lines of energy. Each meridian pathway is connected to a specific organ. Sometimes these points become blocked and, by inserting needles into these specific points, acupuncturists can unblock the qi and restart its flow through the body, rebalancing it.

In Western medicine, acupuncture points are considered as the best places to stimulate nerves, muscles and connective tissues to boost the body's natural pain-management system. However, many believe that acupuncture can also help with anxiety, depression, chronic pain, insomnia, pre-menstrual symptoms, hypertension, migraines and sprains.

An acupuncture session

NOTE: Do not visit an acupuncturist if you have a bleeding disorder, are taking blood thinners or have a pacemaker. Do not have acupuncture performed by anyone who is not a certified, accredited acupuncturist and carry out extensive research on your acupuncturist before booking your appointment. And please, don't try to do acupuncture at home.

A general acupuncture session typically last for about 60–90 minutes, but don't worry, you won't have needles sticking out of your body the whole time. The first half hour of your acupuncture appointment will be dedicated to discussing your symptoms, medical history and any concerns you may have. If this is your first appointment, your acupuncturist may explain the process to you and ease any fears or nerves you may have.

The actual treatment will only last around 30 minutes. Typically, the acupuncturist will put on some calming music and swab each area with alcohol before inserting the needle. The number of needles that may be placed in the body and where depends on your individual needs and comfort level. You may start off with a few needles at your first session and find the acupuncturist adds more at later sessions.

Acupressure

If the thought of getting pricked with thin needles is not your idea of wellness, or you cannot find a licensed acupuncturist in your area, you can still receive all of the benefits of acupuncture, but none of the sharpness, by doing acupressure. Acupressure is similar to acupuncture, but instead of inserting thin needles into your body, you or a practitioner massage specific points to unblock your qi and stimulate the meridians.

Unlike acupuncture, acupressure is something you can perform on yourself, provided that you watch a few videos online and maybe take a class to get you started. Here are a few pressure points to try out, specifically for spiritual healing to help you rebalance your energies and lift you up.

Pressure points for spiritual healing

THE THIRD-EYE POINT: Located just above the bridge of your nose. Lightly touching this spot for a couple minutes each day can enhance your inner awareness. By meditating on this point for a few weeks you'll see an improvement in your natural intuition.

GREAT SURGE LIVER 3: Located on the line between the big toe and the second toe, about three fingers from the edge of the hollow on the top of the foot. Move your index finger counterclockwise on this point for relaxation and to unblock anger.

CONCEPTION VESSEL 17: Located on the centre of the sternum. This pressure point can relieve anxiety, depression, nervousness and other emotional imbalances, as well as boost the immune system. Press the conception vessel 17 with your hands clasped together in prayer. Keep your spine straight.

URINARY BLADDER 10 (B10): Located at the top and back of the neck, just below the base of the skull, about half an inch either side of the neck on the prominent muscles. Pressing these points is good for reducing stress, anxiety, burnout, headache, neck pain and insomnia. It is also good for eye strain.

PALACE OF HEARING (SI-19): Located near the ear just before the front of the ear canal in the depression that forms when you open your mouth. By pressing it for several seconds you can release your inner emotions and desires. However, it is not recommended for everyday use as it's meant for gaining insight only.

GREAT BELL (KI-4): Located on the inside of the foot, near the Achilles tendon and level with the lower part of the ankle bone. Press and release this point several times for 20 seconds to combat fatigue, depression and sluggishness.

YIN PORTALS OF THE FOOT (GB-44): Located on the outer corner of the nail of the fourth toe. By pressing this point you can enhance your ability to make decisions, focus and resolve anger issues.

JOINING OF THE VALLEYS (LI-4): Located on the top of the hand, on the web between thumb and index finger. Squeeze this point to let go of grief and to calm down. **NOTE:** Do not perform this during pregnancy as massaging this point is believed to induce labour.

Chapter Four:

PICKING YOUR PRACTICE

Now that we've looked at the main types of spiritual healing, you may be thinking to yourself, "What do I start with first?" We've gone through so many different methods that the possibilities are endless – and that can be a little overwhelming, especially for a beginner. The best way to start is by doing more research on the types of healing that interest you. What sections did you enjoy the most? Do you have questions about a particular topic? At the end of this book, there is a further reading section, giving you resources to discover more about every topic mentioned in this book.

Remember, you don't have to stick to one form of healing – you can easily incorporate many different types into your life. Just as every person is unique, your healing journey is unique as well, so it's perfectly normal to have a combination of many different practices.

However, if you still can't decide, here are some more things to keep in mind when choosing a practice.

🪷 LOOK AT YOUR HEALTH 🪷

It's important to keep in mind that spiritual healing is not a replacement for doctor's visits, medication or surgeries. Spiritual healing is meant to boost what you're already doing. It's good to talk to your doctor before trying any of these healing methods. This is key because you may have certain medical conditions that do not go well with certain healing practices. These conditions range from allergies, heart conditions, blood disorders and having a pacemaker to being pregnant.

Another reason to talk to a licensed medical professional is that they can give you some tips on how to perform healing safely, despite having pre-existing conditions. For example, if you are interested in doing qigong but have had back surgery, they may be able to give you tips for modified positions, or if you have allergies you can think about ways to use herbalism without actually consuming the herb. They may also be able to provide you with resources, such as the details of a local trusted acupuncturist.

✿ LOCATION ✿

As you start looking into healing practices, keep in mind where you live and what's accessible to you. For example, if you live in a rural area with a big garden, with all that space you could grow plenty of healing herbs, practise qigong or chakra-based yoga outside or study the moon. However, if you live in a big city, it may be easy to find an aura photographer or a healing specialist, but more difficult to plant a full herb garden.

✿ PERSONAL INTERESTS ✿

The easiest way to start your healing practice is by choosing something that fits into an interest or hobby that you already enjoy. For example, if you love fashion or interior decorating then you may enjoy playing with colour healing. If you love working out, qigong may be fun to try. If you are a gardener or a cook, give herbalism a go. And if you just love learning about new cultures, Ayurveda, chakra healing and traditional Chinese medicine would be perfect.

🪷 FINANCIAL INVESTMENT 🪷

While you can't put a price on good health, it's important to look at your budget before seriously committing to certain elements of spiritual healing. This doesn't mean that if you don't have much money it is inaccessible to you. It just means you have to go about it in a different way. For example, if you can't afford acupuncture appointments, learn how to give yourself acupressure massages. If you can't afford a top-of-the-line oil diffuser, look at other, low-cost ways of getting herbs into your life. It doesn't matter if you invest thousands or no money at all into healing – each way can achieve energy balance.

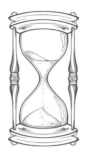

☙ TIME COMMITMENT ☙

With our constantly busy lives, it's easy to look at spiritual healing as something great but inaccessible because it seems like it will take a lot of time out of our day – time that we don't always have. So, look at ways you can incorporate it into your day that don't involve taking up much time at all. Some small ways are drinking herbal tea in the morning or before bed, painting your bedroom or office a certain colour, or reading a few pages of a chakra book every night. Whatever time you can spare for your health is a good thing. Having said that, if you find that you have a lot of time on your hands, feel free to dive right into a very complex subject like TCM.

✿ GOALS ✿

What do you personally want to get out of spiritual healing? Do you want more energy? Do you feel like you are stuck in a rut and you don't how to get out of it? Do you just feel *off* and don't really know why? Write down all the negative feelings you have been living with. Make a note of where you think these symptoms and feelings are coming from. Lastly, write down how you want to feel. By seeing the words on a page it becomes easier to understand your goals and start working toward them.

✿ TRIAL AND ERROR ✿

If you really can't decide on a spiritual healing technique, the best way of discovering what works for you is by giving everything a try. Once you get the go-ahead from your doctor, just try out some things. Some may work for you, some may not. Maybe a combination of things will be best. But as long as you give spiritual healing a shot and come to it with an open mind, you are already taking the first steps to better health.

🪷 A NOTE ON CULTURAL MINDFULNESS 🪷

Whatever practices you end up choosing to use in your life, please remember to practise each healing method with respect and cultural awareness – especially if you are trying a healing method that does not hail from your culture or origin. In recent years the idea of "wellness" has become very trendy, and many of these practices have become commercialized and stripped of their cultural identity. However, this does not mean that you cannot do Ayurveda if you are not of Indian descent; it just means you should do extensive research before trying it out and practise it with respect, acknowledging its roots.

Being mindful and culturally sensitive means you are already creating better energy.

CONCLUSION

Although this is the end of the book, this is only the beginning of your spiritual healing journey. This book is by no means the final word on any of the subjects mentioned here, but just a taste of what the wellness world has to offer you. Take what you have learned here and introduce these healing practices in your own life, in any way that suits your individual needs.

Finally, here are a few mantras to repeat to yourself as you go about your healing. Mantras are sacred utterances that we repeat over and over again to help centre and ground us. They can also be used as positive manifestations, where the more you repeat and visualize positive things, the more likely they are to happen.

- My intuition is always guiding me in the right direction.
- My energy is always flowing.
- Be gentle, be curious.
- I am already healing.

Be well.

✿ FURTHER READING ✿

Moon healing

Ahlquist, Diane *The Moon + You* (2020, Adams Media)

Boland, Yasmin *Moonology* (2016, Hay House)

Herbalism

Chevallier, Andrew *Encyclopedia of Herbal Medicine* (2016, DK)

Murphy-Hiscock, Arin *The Green Witch* (2017, Adams Media)

Chromotherapy

Norris, Stephanie *Secrets of Colour Healing* (2001, DK)

Chakra healing

Alcantara, Margarita *Chakra Healing: A Beginner's Guide to Self-Healing Techniques that Balance the Chakras* (2017, Althea Press)

Perrakis, Athena *The Ultimate Guide to Chakras* (2018, Fair Winds Press)

Pfender, April *Essential Chakra Meditation* (2019, Althea Press)

Reiki

Frazier, Karen *Reiki Healing for Beginners* (2018, Althea Press)

Oula, Valerie *A Little Bit of Reiki* (2019, Sterling)

Ayurveda

Cramer, Ali *Modern Ayurveda* (2019, Althea Press)

Weis-Bohlen, Susan *Ayurveda Beginner's Guide* (2018, Althea Press)

Magnetic healing

Payne, Buryl *Magnetic Healing: Advanced Techniques for the Application of Magnetic Forces* (1999, Lotus Press)

Traditional Chinese medicine

Beinfield, Harriet & Korngold, Efrem *Between Heaven and Earth: A Guide to Chinese Medicine* (1992, Ballantine)

Garran, Thomas Avery *Western Herbs According to Traditional Chinese Medicine* (2008, Healing Arts Press)

Acupuncture/acupressure

Bleecker, Deborah *Acupuncture Points Handbook* (2017, Draycott)

Bleecker, Deborah *Acupressure Made Simple* (2019, Draycott)

Qigong

Cohen, Kenneth S. *The Way of Qigong* (2000, Random House)

Golding, Sophie *Live Better: A Book of Spiritual Guidance* (2017, Summersdale)

General healing

Basile, Lisa Marie *Light Magic for Dark Times* (Fair Winds Press, 2018)

Frazier, Karen *The Little Book of Energy Healing Techniques* (Althea Press, 2019)

If you're interested in finding out more
about our books, find us on Facebook at
SUMMERSDALE PUBLISHERS and follow us
on Twitter at @SUMMERSDALE.

WWW.SUMMERSDALE.COM

IMAGE CREDITS